CITY OF TAMPA, FLORIDA

To order additional copies of this book, contact:
Xlibris
844-714-8691
www.Xlibris.com
Orders@Xlibris.com
823228

CITY OF TAMPA, FLORIDA

FLORIDA

HISTORY ON SIGNS

Ismail Kazem

Introduction

City of Tampa, history on signs is a photographic tour of landmark street signs depicting the fascinating history of the city of Tampa.

Whether you are a visitor or a resident of a city, you have to walk it's streets to observe its identity and explore its neighborhood. The city of Tampa has a dynamic history. AS you stroll down its streets and along its river walk you would appreciate reading the many landmark signs posted on several corners. Each sign tells a story of strife and glory. Of destruction and construction. Of suffering and achievements. All of them bring memories of events and of people who made them. And shed light on the history of your city. A tour of education and enrichment!

Ismail Kazem

1528

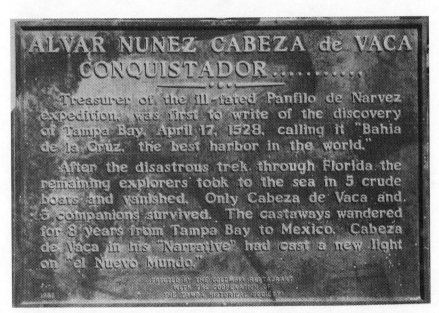

ALVAR NUNEZ CABEZA de VACA
CONQUISTADOR............

Treasurer of the ill-fated Panfilo de Narvez expedition, was first to write of the discovery of Tampa Bay, April 17, 1528, calling it "Bahia de la Cruz, the best harbor in the world."

After the disastrous trek through Florida the remaining explorers took to the sea in 5 crude boats and vanished. Only Cabeza de Vaca and 3 companions survived. The castaways wandered for 8 years from Tampa Bay to Mexico. Cabeza de Vaca in his "Narrative" had cast a new light on "el Nuevo Mundo."

ERECTED BY THE COLUMBIA RESTAURANT
WITH THE COOPERATION OF
THE TAMPA HISTORICAL SOCIETY

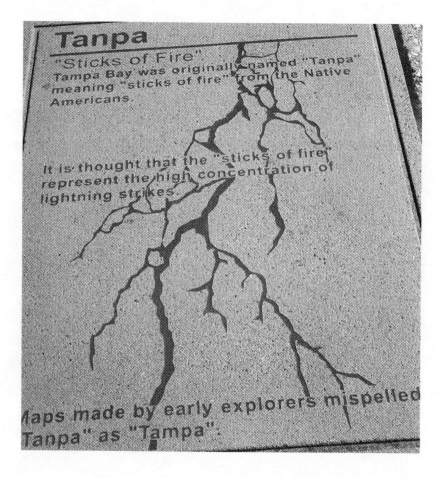

Tanpa

"Sticks of Fire"
Tampa Bay was originally named "Tanpa" meaning "sticks of fire" from the Native Americans.

It is thought that the "sticks of fire" represent the high concentration of lightning strikes.

Maps made by early explorers misspelled "Tanpa" as "Tampa".

Upland Habitat

Trees:
Live Oak, Laurel Oak, Sabal Palm, Magnolia, Red Cedar, American Holly, Redbay, Slash Pine

Shrubs:
Saw Palmetto, Yaupon Holly, Coontie, Coral Honeysuckle, Beautyberry

Live Oak
Quercus virginiana

Slash Pine
Pinus elliottii

Saw Palmetto
Serenoa repens

The Shore

a convergence of land, water, natural forces and life, forming a rich habitat and ever-changing ecosystem. The native shoreline in this area was thought to be about where the centerline of "Ice Palace Drive" lies.

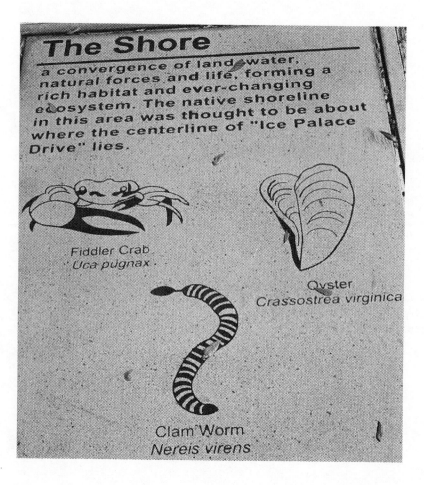

Fiddler Crab
Uca pugnax

Oyster
Crassostrea virginica

Clam Worm
Nereis virens

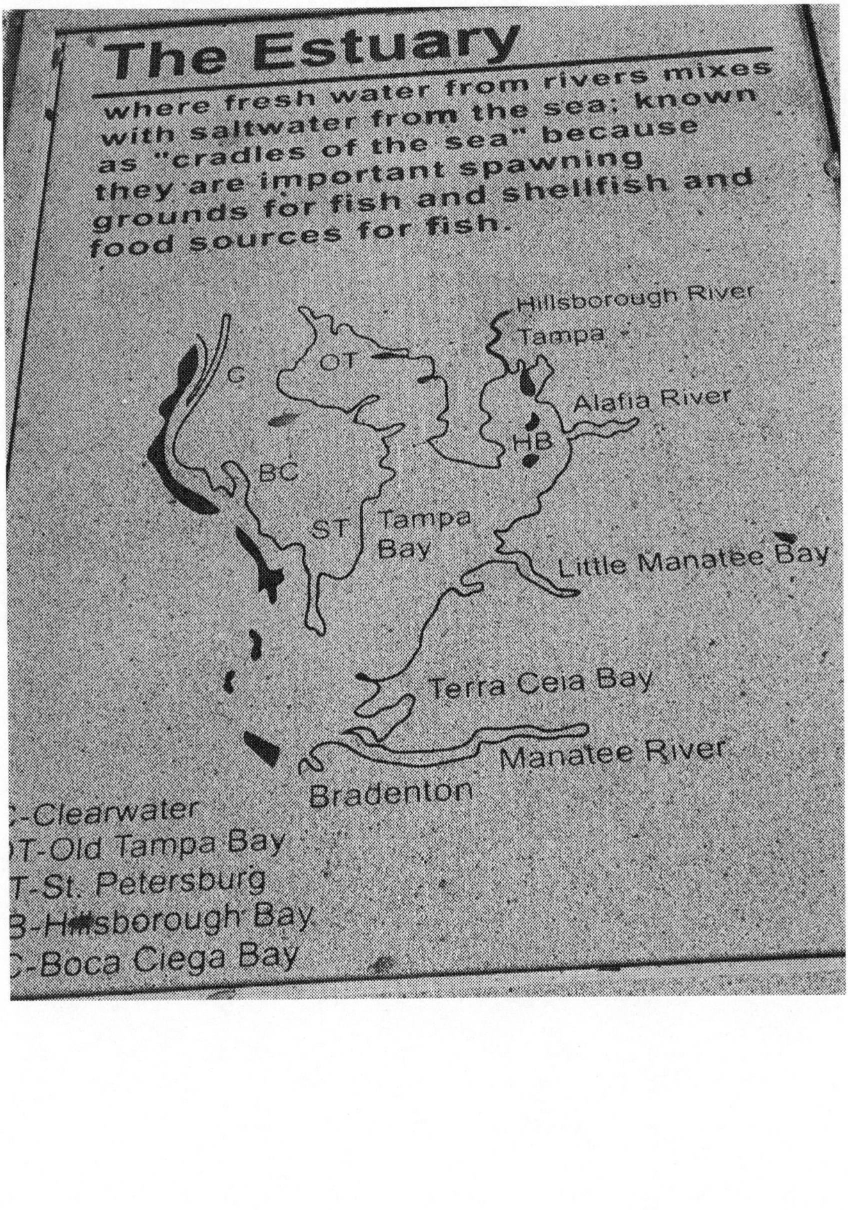

The Estuary

where fresh water from rivers mixes with saltwater from the sea; known as "cradles of the sea" because they are important spawning grounds for fish and shellfish and food sources for fish.

Hillsborough River
Tampa
Alafia River
Little Manatee Bay
Terra Ceia Bay
Manatee River
Bradenton
Tampa Bay
OT
G
BC
ST
HB

C-Clearwater
OT-Old Tampa Bay
ST-St. Petersburg
HB-Hillsborough Bay
BC-Boca Ciega Bay

The Mangrove

the Native Americans called the Red Mangrove "The Walking Tree" because of its prop roots. The prop roots help stabilize soil-helping to 'create land' and shelter young and small sealife.

Red Mangrove

The Marsh

the Saltmarsh and Smooth Cordgrasses help bind the soil and provide substrate and food for sealife. The grasses are also cold-hardy. In years that lack major freezes, the Mangroves become dominant, otherwise the marsh grasses are the prominent species.

Spartina alterniflora / Smooth Cordgrass
Spartina bakeri / Sand Cordgrass
Spartina patens / Salt Marsh Cordgrass

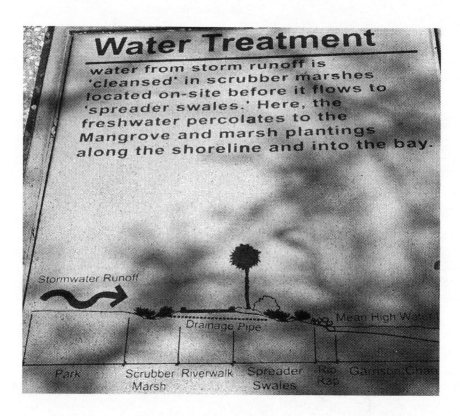

Water Treatment

water from storm runoff is 'cleansed' in scrubber marshes located on-site before it flows to 'spreader swales.' Here, the freshwater percolates to the Mangrove and marsh plantings along the shoreline and into the bay.

Stormwater Runoff

Drainage Pipe

Mean High Water

Park   Scrubber Riverwalk   Spreader   Rip   Garrison Chan
        Marsh   Swales   Rap

The Wildlife

Shoreline Birds:
Herons, Pelicans, Gulls, Ospreys, Coots, Anhingas, Terns, Spoonbill

Fish:
Sheepshead, Snook, Redfish, Seatrout, Mullet, Mangrove Snapper

Great Blue Heron

Brown Pelican

Roseate Spoonbill

Snook

Red Drum

Sheepshead

Tampa & Cotanchobee

The word *Tampa*, from which Tampa derives its modern name, was used for hundreds, & perhaps, thousands of years before the coming of Europeans to these shores. It was the name of a nearby Indian village. When the Spaniards arrived, at least by 1513, this lower southwest shoreline was a focus of their explorations. They heard the Natives using this word, & the Spaniards wrote it in their documents. They did not understand it, & no dependable translation survives, but its use today echoes that rich and exciting history. Another way in which the Natives distinguished this area was by its topography. They called it *cotan chobi*, a contraction of the phrase *cotani chobi*, "the big place where the water meets the land." In English, we write their words "Cotanchobee." Here, the beautiful river that we know today as the Hillsborough sweeps gracefully to it's wide, deep bay, before merging with the Gulf of Mexico. How many Natives occupied this land before the Europeans found it? We will never know for sure but, certainly, thousands or even hundreds of thousands of men, women, and children lived here or traveled across this rich land. Where you stand now, they passed their lives: they walked, ate, slept, worked, loved, & died here. Consider how much this land has meant to all of its inheritors.

Cotanchobee & Tampa

Today's Tampa was a war town, born of the conflict between the bold, young United States & the Native peoples for control of the land & its tremendous resources. The Spanish Crown relinquished control of *La Florida* for the first time in 1763. The British, overlords for a short 21 years between the 1st & 2nd Spanish Occupations, created two Floridas, East & West, for administrative purposes. Then, they left in 1784, with the end of the American Revolution, & returned the land to the Spaniards. But, by 1810, partly as a result of the Louisiana Purchase, the northern & western borders of "the Floridas" had been defined & the new United States wanted the area, with its long, strategic shore line. In 1821, "Florida" became a single U.S. Territory, with the shape that we know so well today. The numbers of Euroamerican & African American settlers & slaves streaming into Florida began to increase rapidly. In 1813-14, the Native peoples of Alabama had risen up against the white settlers & had been defeated badly by Andrew Jackson. Several thousand of those warriors & their families moved southward & joined their cultural kinfolk, whom English speakers called the Seminoles & Miccosukees, across the interior & along the shores of what Americans now called Tampa Bay. Once again, the stage was set for conflict over Florida's vast land & resources, & Tampa would have yet another name – Fort Brooke, as well as a central role in the coming drama that would be played out across Florida.

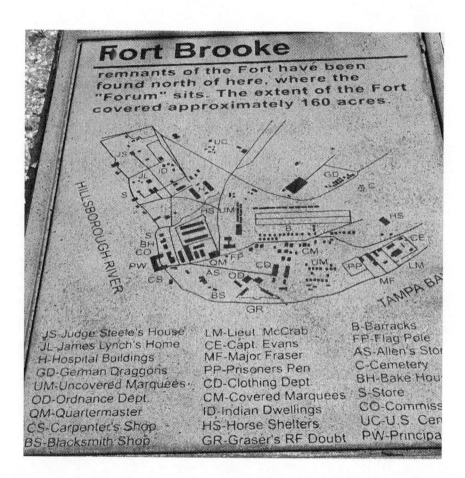

Fort Brooke

remnants of the Fort have been found north of here, where the "Forum" sits. The extent of the Fort covered approximately 160 acres.

JS-Judge Steele's House
JL-James Lynch's Home
H-Hospital Buildings
GD-German Draggons
UM-Uncovered Marquees
OD-Ordnance Dept.
QM-Quartermaster
CS-Carpenter's Shop
BS-Blacksmith Shop

LM-Lieut. McCrab
CE-Capt. Evans
MF-Major Fraser
PP-Prisoners Pen
CD-Clothing Dept.
CM-Covered Marquees
ID-Indian Dwellings
HS-Horse Shelters
GR-Graser's RF Doubt

B-Barracks
FP-Flag Pole
AS-Allen's Stor
C-Cemetery
BH-Bake Hou
S-Store
CO-Commiss
UC-U.S. Cen
PW-Principa

12

Harriet Axtell, the daughter of Presbyterian minister Henry Axtell who served as Fort Brooke's chaplain, wrote the following excerpt describing Fort Brooke in 1845:

[Fort Brooke] is a quiet little place, with sufficient noise and bustle, occasioned by the customary avocations of a soldier's life in which all take and feel an interest... To the south of the cantonment the land stretches round a point which juts into the bay. This promontory is covered with a growth composed of mangrove, Pine and Cabbage Trees... The opposite bank slopes to the water, and is generally covered with wild flowers. The scenery beyond is diversified, consisting of Pine trees, with here and there a hammock of moss, or a swamp shadowed by elder bushes, and white with feathery blossoms of the swamp grass.

The garrison consists of twenty houses arranged in fanciful order, among the old live oak trees hanging with moss. It lies lengthwise from north to south and is about seven furlongs in length [with each furlong equaling 220 yards], and four or five in width, or east to west. The eye first rests on the parade, which is set out with lime and orange trees... This grove is enclosed with a white picket fence, of three feet high: in the center stands a pavilion with a round platform supporting a roof and columns, under this is a wall tent where the garrison library is kept.

Tampa Bay & Fort Brooke

It was Gen. Andrew Jackson who recommended that a fort be built on Tampa Bay. James Gadsden, his aide, suggested that troops from the Fourth Infantry should be the first to be stationed at the new post. Col. George Mercer Brooke, a hero of the War of 1812, commanded a unit of the Fourth, which was stationed at Pensacola. Col. Brooke arrived at the Tampa Bay site on Jan. 22, 1824, with four companies. The fort that he designed had utility, convenience, & beauty. Capt. Isaac Clark, a military comrade, pronounced the barracks with its setting among majestic live oaks & wild orange trees, "The best barracks of its kind, in the United States." A visitor found the site "delightful." Beyond the beauty of its location, Cantonment Brooke – soon, Fort Brooke, would become the southern anchor of the U.S. military line of offense & control that would be anchored on the northeast by Fort King, at the Indian Agency, near the site of the old Indian village of *Ocale* (Ocala, "my camp"). In proposing the fort on the bay, Gadsden had told the Secretary of War that "a judicious location of an adequate force simultaneous with the concentration of the Indians cannot but have the happy effect of obtaining such a control as to render them perfectly Subservient to the views of the Government." In this, he was echoing the view of many in government, but not of the military officers on the scene. The soldiers knew that the Florida Indians had no intention of becoming "perfectly Subservient" to anyone.

Fort Brooke & Tampa

Throughout the 2nd & 3rd Seminole Wars (1835-42; 1856-58), Fort Brooke served as the nucleus of a small but growing community that included not only soldiers of many ethnic backgrounds & languages, but also settlers, slaves, & Freedmen lured by the military economy, as well as by all of the excellent features of terrain & climate that continue to attract residents & visitors today. Among the troops were many foreign-born men for whom military enlistment provided fast & easy entry into the new society, although service in the heat, mosquitoes, & snakes of Florida would not seem easy at all. An Englishman, John Bemrose, who served as a hospital orderly at several Florida forts, recorded that he met Germans, French, Scots, Polish, Swedes, Canadians, & Nova Scotians. Their languages seemed to him "like the chatter of Babel." The Indians visited the fort to obtain supplies. Indian prisoners & emigrants encamped here, awaiting transport. The long shoreline of Cotanchobee also made a fine meeting place for Cuban fishermen who secretly brought in arms & ammunition to support the Indian resisters. In Jan. 1834, Hillsborough became Florida's 18th county, & its seat was named for Tampa, the settlement that had taken root around Fort Brooke. The fort remained active until it was formally abandoned by the U.S. government on Dec. 21, 1882. It was occupied regularly until 1860 &, thereafter, was a seasonal camp for soldiers from Key West Barracks.

The U.S. & the Indians

The 19th-century conflicts recorded in U.S. history as the 1st, 2nd, & 3rd Seminole Wars were, in reality, part of a much larger & longer clash of cultures. Since its own birth, in conflict, the U.S. had wrestled with "the Indian problem." Although the tribes were recognized as sovereign nations &, therefore, independent actors in this international drama, the continuous population growth & ever-expanding settlement of the new "Americans" spawned almost a century of Wars of Indian Removal that were destined to end, finally, at Fort Brooke, Florida, the Indians' Cotanchobee, in 1858. From the Iroquois in the north, to the Cherokees in the Carolinas &, finally, to the Seminoles in Florida, the U.S. fought the Indians over control of land. In 1813 U.S. soldiers had crossed an international border to burn Indian towns in Spanish Florida. In 1817-18, Andrew Jackson entered Spanish Florida & destroyed Indian towns, crops, & livestock, in the 1st Seminole War. By the Treaty of Moultrie Creek (near St. Augustine), in 1823, the Florida tribes were confined to a reservation in the interior of the peninsula, but getting them to go there was another problem entirely. Supplying them with promised foodstuffs was yet another. A military fortification, to be constructed on Tampa Bay, would permit the U.S. government to get promised supplies to the Indians & also would defend against Cuban Spaniards who might supply their old Indian friends with arms & ammunition.

Fort Brooke & the Indians

When the U.S. acquired Florida, in 1821, the policy of the U.S. government still favored making treaties & attempting to buy Indian lands. Within a decade, however, the situation changed dramatically. Gen. Andrew Jackson became President Jackson. The Indian Removal Act (1830) made it official policy that any future treaties would require the Natives to move to the newly created "Indian Territory" west of the Mississippi River. The situation of the Florida Indians already had been worsened significantly by the Treaty of Moultrie Creek (1823), which restricted them to poor, wet, & unproductive lands in the center of the peninsula. The military authorities tried to restrict liquor dealers from the reservation, but with little success. Some settlers, desirous of Indian lands & the economic upturn that a military presence would bring, disguised themselves as Indians & attacked their own neighbors in order to justify a call for a military buildup. Promised supplies did not arrive on time; the Indians' planting & harvesting cycles were disrupted; & starvation became a real possibility. The Treaty of Payne's Landing (on the St. John's River), forced upon the Florida Indians in 1832, was strictly a Removal treaty. The determination of the U.S. government to enforce this treaty would precipitate the longest & most costly Indian war in U.S. history. The entire fighting system of the U.S. Army, Navy, & Marine Corps would change because of the experiences of the soldiers at Fort Brooke & other Florida forts during the Seminole Wars of Removal.

War Years: the U.S.

The Wars of Indian Removal in Florida were national, rather than merely regional, events. Americans who, early in the war, supported forcing the Indians out of the path of white settlement, lost interest as fighting dragged on with no clear victories or defeats. The cost of the war mounted steadily, with only relatively few prisoners to show for the effort. Reports to families from husbands, brothers, & uncles in the field were very mixed. Some saw the hills, hammocks, & richness of the foliage and thought Florida an Eden. Most could barely stand it. One soldier wrote home: "If the Devil owned both Hell and Florida, he would rent out Florida and live in Hell!" Even the scenic beauty of Fort Brooke could not compensate for the heat, mosquitoes, snakes, & the maddening humidity. Enlisted men earned only $5 per month. Desertion was a constant problem. Besides the Indians & the climate, the terrain was the enemy as well. Much Florida coastal land was still swamp & even the highland pine barrens were clogged with palmettos & dense undergrowth. Marching quietly & easily was impossible. Fighting was suspended during the summer's "sickly season," but malaria & dysentery shadowed the soldiers nonetheless. This situation was only worsened by the fact that the Indians had the distinct advantage of fighting on their own territory. European linear tactics were of little use against an enemy that appeared & disappeared at will, fighting 'hit-&-run' style & melting into the trees and swamps. U.S. soldiers at Fort Brooke were fighting America's first 'guerilla' war.

Years of Conflict

Throughout its existence, Fort Brooke retained its prominence in the U.S. military's offensive operations in Florida. Below present-day Whiting St., there were horse sheds, a bake house, a carpenter's shop, a Quartermaster's store, a "pen" for Indian prisoners, a hospital, & a cemetery. Nine overall commanders would take the field in Florida, & most of them would visit the fort at one time or another. Among them were Gen., later President, Zachary Taylor, Gen. Thos. S. Jesup, & Lt. Col. William Harney. Soldiers of all ranks, from privates to generals, would gain military experience here that would propel them to advancement in their nation's later 19th-century wars: the Mexican War, the Civil War, & the U.S. wars against the western, Plains, Indians. The Fort Brooke reservation, 4 miles square, reached the zenith of its occupation in late 1837, when 65 officers & 1,596 enlisted men were in garrison. Over the last year, 450 Indians had been gathered at the fort, awaiting transport to the West. Others continued to come in or be captured. On June 2, 1837, Osceola & Abiaka & a war party of about 200, released the prisoners. Gen. Jesup was disheartened. "This campaign, so far as relates to Indian migration," he wrote, "has entirely failed." In Oct. 1837, a number of Indian war leaders were captured, & the fort's garrison was reduced, even as the war dragged on for another five years. The U.S. withdrew from Florida in 1842, ending the 2nd Seminole War, & Congress passed the Armed Occupation Act, encouraging white settlement of the Florida frontier.

War Years: the Indians

U.S. warfare, based on the European model, required confrontation: two armies must oppose each other on open land. But the Indians fought in small, flexible units, under individual war leaders chosen for the occasion by the war council. When the council decided upon a series of preemptive strikes against the U.S., late in 1835, they believed that the U.S. would see their power & resolve, & leave them alone. They did not realize that, in the eyes of the white government, they had issued a challenge that would bring down upon them the entire military might of the U.S. The opening gambit was the destruction of a column of 108 men, marching from Fort Brooke to Fort King, under the command of Maj. Francis Dade, on Dec. 28, 1835. For the next seven years, at least one sixth of every graduating class from the U.S. Military Academy at West Point would be posted directly to Florida to fight the Indians. Over 10,000 regular soldiers, sailors, & Marines, plus 30,000 citizen soldiers, would pass through the Territory & (from 1845) the State. Twice, in 1842 & 1858, the U.S. would simply withdraw from the conflict, without benefit of treaty. The terrain & the will favored the Indians. Manpower &, sometimes, arms, favored the U.S. Ultimately, only slightly over 3,000 Indian men, women, & children, plus their ex-slave & Freedmen dependents, were removed from Florida. The U.S. believed that the remaining few hundred Indians never would be able to survive. Once again, they were mistaken.

The Fort & Town of Tampa

Above Whiting St. & the military reservation, the town of Tampa was taking shape even as the wars continued. First came those who provided skills useful to the military: cobblers, harness makers, laundresses, blacksmiths, among others. Sometimes their families came as well. Among the officers & men who appreciated the intensity of Florida's climate & landscape, some stayed on after their service, as merchants or government agents. Throughout the wars, & years of intermittent raids & skirmishes, the Indians continued to visit Fort Brooke & Tampa also, to trade or fish, or conduct other business. The Indians had made it clear all along that their fight was not with individuals but, rather, with a government that would go so far as to kill them in order to take away their homes. But the withdrawal of troops in 1842 angered & frightened many Floridians, & tensions mounted again, until they erupted in a short series of skirmishes that constituted the 3rd Seminole War (1856-58). U.S. soldiers destroyed a camp & garden belonging to Billy Bowlegs, & the Indians fought back. For the second time, however, the U.S. made a unilateral decision to pull its troops out. The cost of removing the few hundred remaining Seminoles would far outweigh the benefits. They would finally be left alone in their homeland. The tiny community of Tampa would remain also, until the coming of Henry Plant's railroad, in the late 19th-century, would provide a distinct economic base for municipal growth.

"They are taking us beyond Miami,
They are taking us beyond the Caloosa River,
They are taking us to the end of our Tribe,
They are taking us to Palm Beach,
Coming back beside Lake Okeechobee,
They are taking us to an old town in the West."

"We are going with Washington [*government*].
What boat do we get in?"
Seminole Laments

The years following 1858, the end of the 3rd, & last, of the Seminole Wars were times of sad reorganization for Florida's Indians. Their families had been torn apart, their ceremonial cycles had been disrupted, & their agricultural base had been destroyed. In their main objective, however, they had been successful. Those few hundred of the people who had fought so valiantly to remain had found refuge in the wild & harsh Everglades, where no others dared venture. They were profoundly weary, but they were alive, & still in their homeland. By the 1880s they would once again return to Tampa, to the Cotanchobee of their ancestors. They would meet white settlers in peace asking, once again, only to be left alone to live their lives. This time, they would find understanding.

Years of Removal

The entire U.S. watched the Florida struggle, & the names of the war leaders became household words. Today, towns, cities, & landmarks across the nation, for example, as well as numerous individuals, are named for Osceola (*Asse yahola*) one the young firebrands of the resistance. But Micanopy (*Mikkó mópi*), Philip (*Emáthla*), Billy Bowlegs (*Holata mikkó*), & Sam Jones (*Abiáka*), were among the more powerful official leaders of the wars. Micanopy & Philip were captured & sent West in 1838, along with the family of Osceola, who had died in prison at Fort Moultrie, SC. Bowlegs, the last to give up, left Tampa Bay on the steamer *Grey Cloud*, bound for New Orleans & on to Indian Territory, in 1858. Old Jumper (*Oti emáthla*), & the younger warrior Wildcat (*Coacochi*) were sent West also. Jumper died en route, at New Orleans Barracks, but Wildcat lived to increase his fame as a warrior. Sam Jones, a powerful medicine man & the backbone of the resistance, told the U.S. that he would never give up, as long as he had "a single ball and charge of powder." When he could no longer shoot, he declared, he would "live on fish" &, when his lines were worn out, he would "make others of horse hair" &, when his hooks were worn out, he would "cut up his old tin pans & make others." Sam Jones & his followers found safety in the Everglades & he died there, true to his word never to give up his fight. To this day, the Florida Seminoles pass these names down among the warriors' descendents, & name children with words from the old war-

The Relocation Journey
From Tampa, Florida to Seminole, Oklahoma

This map depicts the route taken by many Indigenous Peoples during their relocation. According to the Seminole Emigration Records, the Seminoles were usually collected at Tampa Bay, Florida and from there taken to New Orleans, Louisiana and then to Fort Gibson, Indian Territory where they were officially recorded as having "arrived" west.

"3,000 Seminole Indians, including many Seminole War Leaders, were captured in various ways, some even under a flag of truce. They were then exiled from Tampa, Florida to Indian Territory.

The Seminole Spirit lives on after 175 years of being removed from homelands in the Southeast, most notably Florida. Culture, tradition, and American lifestyles

1840

TIMUQUAN INDIAN MOUND

Near this site on the shore of the bay, once stood a large Timuquan Temple Mound dating before the time of Christ. It was 50 feet in height with a large level space on top where elaborately decorated temples and residences of Indian chiefs and shamans had stood.

The Fort Brooke soldiers, in the 1840's, used a tall Gumbo Limbo tree growing at the crest of the city-block long mound as a lookout post. The ladies of the post enjoyed ice cream parties at the summit in a beautiful Chinese pavilion.

After the Army withdrew in 1882, the mound was razed to fill the Jackson Street ditch which extended from Marion Street to the river.

ERECTED BY THE TIMUQUANIAN SOCIETY, INC. WITH THE COOPERATION OF THE TAMPA HISTORICAL SOCIETY

1818

OFFICERS QUARTERS
FORT BROOKE

MAJ. GEN. ANDREW JACKSON
(The Provisional Governor of Florida)
(7th President of the United States)
First Recommended This Area As A
Military Site In 1818
(established 1824)
During the 1st Seminole Indian War

BRIG. GEN. ZACHARY TAYLOR
(12th President of the United States)
Commanded From Here. 1838-1840,
the U. S. Army
In 2nd Seminole Indian War

1846

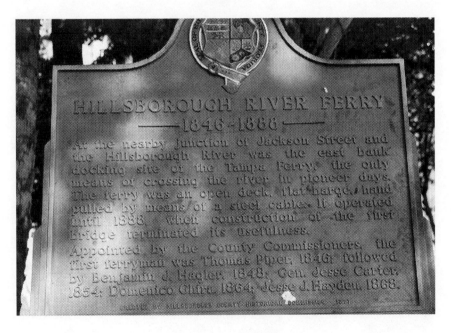

1848

CAPT. JAMES McKAY, I (1808-1876)

On this site, after the devastating hurricane of 1848, McKay, a native of Scotland, built his first permanent home of finished lumber from Mobile, Ala. Here, with his wife Matilda, they raised their children.

McKay was a dominant factor in the upbuilding of Tampa in pioneer times. His shipping lines established the first commercial connection with the outside world. In 1848, he built a courthouse; in 1858, opened the first cattle trade with Cuba, and in 1859, was elected Mayor.

During the Civil War, with his sidewheeler, the Scottish Chief, he became one of Florida's most active blockade-runners; also formed the "Cowboy Cavalry" to protect cattle drives headed for the war-front.

ERECTED BY THE TAMPA HISTORICAL SOCIETY

1850

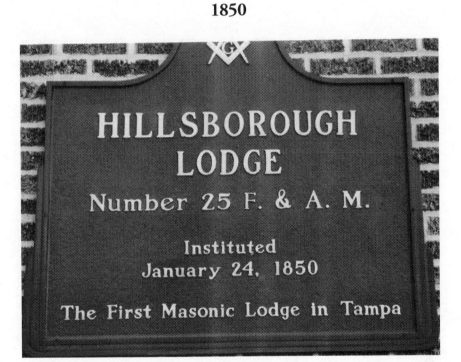

1851

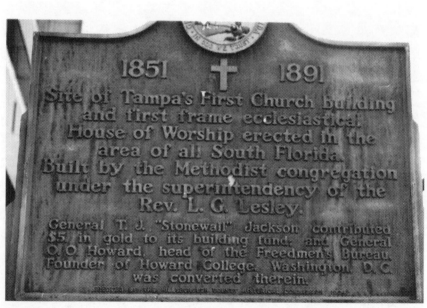

1871

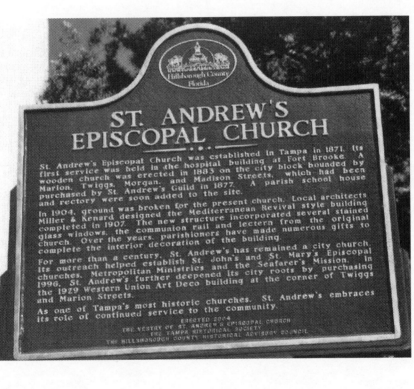

1883

FORT BROOKE CEMETERY

During the Second Seminole War (1835-42) the U. S. Army established a cemetery at this site for soldiers, civilian employees, and Indians.

In 1883, about 20 soldiers were removed to Barrancas National Cemetery, Pensacola. In time the grave sites became obliterated, and passed out of all remembrance.

In 1980, the burial site was discovered accidentally during the construction of the city parking complex. One hundred and two soldiers and civilians were reburied at Oaklawn Cemetery, March 24, 1981, while the spirit of 42 Seminoles were put to rest with the essence of burning herbs at the Seminole Shrine at Orient Road, August 5, 1981.

ERECTED BY THE TAMPA HISTORICAL SOCIETY

1888

1898

THE ROUGH RIDERS
PASSED BY HERE

On June 3, 1898, when Tampa was a cluster of
old weather beaten houses floating on an ocean
of sand, Teddy Roosevelt and the Rough Riders
disembarked from their seven train convoy in
Ybor City, five miles from Tampa City Hall.
They commandeered some wagons, and moved
men, material and animals, through this inter-
section to their encampment on the Tampa Bay
Hotel Road, about one mile west of the river.
The Rough Riders who "could whip Caesar's Tenth
Legion," brought enduring fame to Tampa.

ERECTED BY THE FIRST U. S. VOLUNTEER CAVALRY REGIMENT - ROUGH RIDERS, INC.
HISTORICAL COMMITTEE, DR. JAS. W. COVINGTON, TONY PIZZO & HAMPTON DUNN

1848 - 1891

COURTHOUSE SQUARE

For 104 years this block was the official site of executive and judicial government for Hillsborough County, Florida. The first courthouse, a log building burned by Seminole Indians in 1836, possibly stood here. Subsequent ones were built on this square in 1848, 1855 and 1891. The latter a unique red brick, silver domed building, designed by J. A. Wood, architect of H. B. Plant's famed Tampa Bay Hotel, was demolished in 1952.

TAMPA HISTORICAL SOCIETY
IN COOPERATION WITH
MARINE BANK AND TRUST CO.

1891

1893

1898

TAMPA BAY HOTEL

On June 14, 1898, Lt. Col. Theodore Roosevelt and the First United States Volunteer Cavalry, known as Rough Riders, embarked from Port Tampa for victory in the Spanish-American War. The Tampa Bay Hotel was used as headquarters for general officers who came to organize an invasion force for Cuba, and it gained national attention. Lt. Col. Roosevelt and his wife, Edith Kermit Carow Roosevelt, were hotel guests for a brief stay. Later, Colonel Theodore Roosevelt became the 26th President of the United States of America 1901-1909.

NATIONAL SOCIETY COLONIAL DAMES XVII CENTURY
EDMUND SHEFFIELD CHAPTER 1992

1902

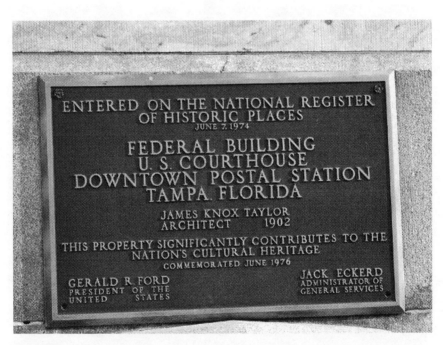

1909

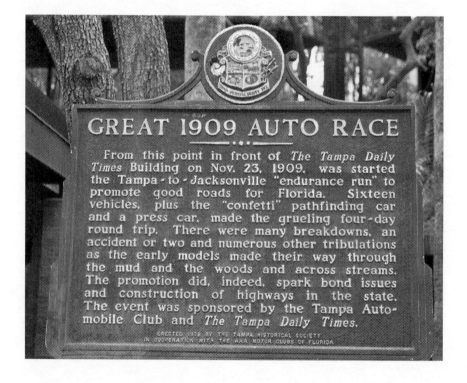

GREAT 1909 AUTO RACE

From this point in front of *The Tampa Daily Times* Building on Nov. 23, 1909, was started the Tampa-to-Jacksonville "endurance run" to promote good roads for Florida. Sixteen vehicles, plus the "confetti" pathfinding car and a press car, made the grueling four-day round trip. There were many breakdowns, an accident or two and numerous other tribulations as the early models made their way through the mud and the woods and across streams. The promotion did, indeed, spark bond issues and construction of highways in the state. The event was sponsored by the Tampa Automobile Club and *The Tampa Daily Times*.

ERECTED 1978 BY THE TAMPA HISTORICAL SOCIETY
IN COOPERATION WITH THE AAA MOTOR CLUBS OF FLORIDA

1911

MEMORIA IN AETERNA, 1911
HILLSBOROUGH COUNTY'S
CONFEDERATE MONUMENT

location in 1952 following completion of the new Hillsborough County Courthouse. In 1996, Hillsborough County collaborated with the National Institute for the Conservation of Cultural Property, Save our Sculpture, to assess the condition of this prominent sculpture. The County completed the thorough cleaning and conservation treatment, but did not restore the broken rifles in order to maintain the original integrity of the historic piece. The Confederate Battle Flag is depicted on the front of the work and the dates 1861 and 1865 refer to the beginning and ending of the War Between the States. The poem on the east side was written by Sister Esther Carlotta, a Roman Catholic nun who was president of the Florida Division of the United Daughters of the Confederacy in 1911. The soldier facing north has been interpreted as the determined warrior facing the invader at the beginning of the war, while the heroic youth facing south is seen returning home from the conflict in a tattered uniform, wounded but not forgotten.

ERECTED 1997 BY THE TAMPA HISTORICAL SOCIETY;
TAMPA CHAPTER NO.113, UNITED DAUGHTERS OF THE CONFEDERACY;
AND JAMES B. HAYWARD, COMMANDER, JOHN T. LESLEY CAMP NO.1282,
SONS OF CONFEDERATE VETERANS

1911

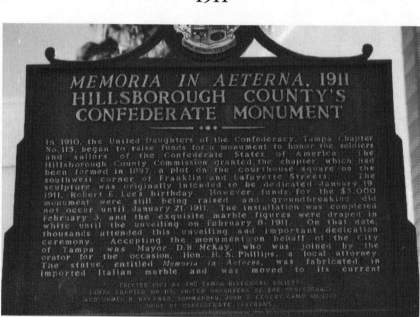

MEMORIA IN AETERNA, 1911
HILLSBOROUGH COUNTY'S
CONFEDERATE MONUMENT

In 1910, the United Daughters of the Confederacy, Tampa Chapter No. 113, began to raise funds for a monument to honor the soldiers and sailors of the Confederate States of America. The Hillsborough County Commission granted the chapter, which had been formed in 1897, a plot on the courthouse square on the southwest corner of Franklin and Lafayette Streets. The sculpture was originally intended to be dedicated January 19, 1911, Robert E. Lee's birthday. However, funds for the $3,000 monument were still being raised and groundbreaking did not occur until January 21, 1911. The installation was completed February 3, and the exquisite marble figures were draped in white until the unveiling on February 8, 1911. On that date, thousands attended this unveiling and important dedication ceremony. Accepting the monument on behalf of the City of Tampa was Mayor D.H. McKay, who was joined by the orator for the occasion, Hon. H.S. Phillips, a local attorney. The statue, entitled *Memoria In Aeterna*, was fabricated in imported Italian marble and was moved to its current

1917-1918

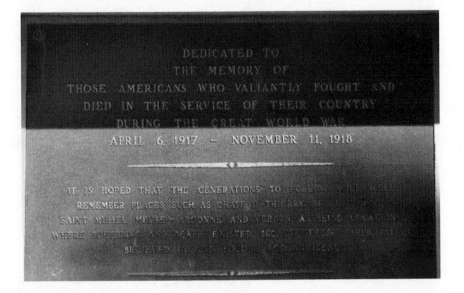

DEDICATED TO
THE MEMORY OF
THOSE AMERICANS WHO VALIANTLY FOUGHT AND
DIED IN THE SERVICE OF THEIR COUNTRY
DURING THE GREAT WORLD WAR
APRIL 6, 1917 – NOVEMBER 11, 1918

IT IS HOPED THAT THE GENERATIONS TO FOLLOW WILL ALWAYS
REMEMBER PLACES SUCH AS CHATEAU-THIERRY, BELLEAU WOOD,
SAINT MIHIEL, MEUSE-ARGONNE AND VERDUN, AS BEING LOCATION
WHERE SUFFERING AND DEATH EXISTED BECAUSE THOSE PARTICIPATING
BELIEVED IN THE FREEDOM FOR ALL MEN.

1941-1946

DEDICATED TO
THE MEMORY OF
THOSE AMERICANS WHO FOUGHT AND GAVE THEIR
LIVES IN EUROPE, AFRICA, THE PACIFIC, AND ASIA IN THE
DEFENSE OF THEIR COUNTRY DURING WORLD WAR II
DECEMBER 7 1941 – DECEMBER 31 1946

LET IT BE KNOWN AMERICANS GALLANTLY FOUGHT AND DIED
FROM PEARL HARBOR, BATAAN–CORREGIDOR NORTH AFRICA SALERNO
NORMANDY CORAL SEA GUADALCANAL THE BULGE AND
IWO JIMA TO HIROSHIMA DETERMINED THAT
TYRANNY AND ANARCHY SHOULD NOT PREVAIL

THE GOLD STAR MEMORIAL REGISTRY
IS IN THE COURT HOUSE BUILDING

1950

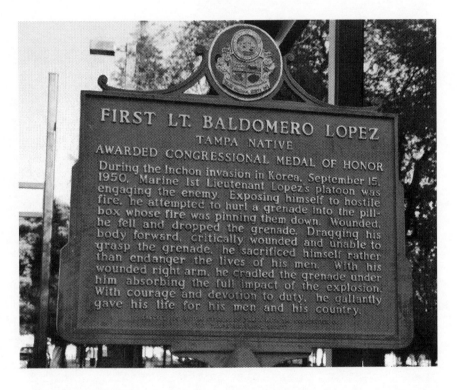

FIRST LT. BALDOMERO LOPEZ
TAMPA NATIVE
AWARDED CONGRESSIONAL MEDAL OF HONOR
During the Inchon invasion in Korea, September 15,
1950, Marine 1st Lieutenant Lopez's platoon was
engaging the enemy. Exposing himself to hostile
fire, he attempted to hurl a grenade into the pill-
box whose fire was pinning them down. Wounded,
he fell and dropped the grenade. Dragging his
body forward, critically wounded and unable to
grasp the grenade, he sacrificed himself rather
than endanger the lives of his men. With his
wounded right arm, he cradled the grenade under
him absorbing the full impact of the explosion.
With courage and devotion to duty, he gallantly
gave his life for his men and his country.

1982

RECOGNIZING SUPPORT FOR THE 1982
PRESERVATION, RESTORATION, AND
BEAUTIFICATION OF PLANT PARK

CITY OF TAMPA
BOB MARTINEZ, MAYOR

FEDERAL FUNDS ALLOCATED FROM THE
HERITAGE CONSERVATION AND RECREATION
SERVICE OF THE U.S. DEPARTMENT OF
THE INTERIOR. FUNDS ADMINISTERED BY
THE DIVISION OF ARCHIVES, HISTORY,
AND RECORDS MANAGEMENT OF THE
FLORIDA DEPARTMENT OF STATE

DESIGNER
CITY OF TAMPA PARKS DEPARTMENT

1984

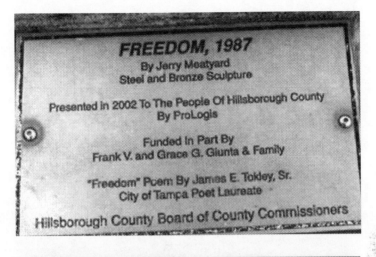

FREEDOM, 1987
By Jerry Meatyard
Steel and Bronze Sculpture

Presented In 2002 To The People Of Hillsborough County
By ProLogis

Funded In Part By
Frank V. and Grace G. Giunta & Family

"Freedom" Poem By James E. Tokley, Sr.
City of Tampa Poet Laureate

Hillsborough County Board of County Commissioners

Gaze at me and wonder what I see
My arms, outstretched, that measure countless stars
My stance unmatched by even the tallest tree
The compass of my feet, a common cause!
O gaze at me and wonder what you see
My glistening chest that hides a heart of steel
That judges Human Will and finds it free
To reach aloft and spin God's cosmic wheel!
To make of life whatever life may be,
Like an early morning sun, I rise up free!

1996

CHARLES J. JAEGER AND JOAN ZACHARELLIS
HYDRIA 1996
CONCRETE CISTERN
21' x 10' x 10'

COMMISSIONED BY THE
HILLSBOROUGH COUNTY BOARD OF COUNTY COMMISSIONERS
THROUGH ITS PUBLIC ART PROGRAM IN COLLABORATION WITH
SOUTHWEST FLORIDA WATER MANAGEMENT DISTRICT

SINCE ANCIENT GREEK TIMES, CIRCA 1200 B.C., CITIZENS
HAVE BUILT CISTERNS TO COLLECT AND STORE WATER.
THOUSANDS OF CISTERNS ARE STILL IN USE THROUGHOUT
THE WORLD. HOMES EQUIPPED WITH CISTERNS CONSERVE
VALUABLE WATER.

HYDRIA, TAKEN FROM THE GREEK WORD FOR WATER JAR
STORES ABOUT 15,000 GALLONS OF RAIN WATER IN THE
COLUMNS AND AN UNDERGROUND TANK FOR REUSE IN
THE COURTHOUSE IRRIGATION SYSTEM. LANDSCAPING
INCORPORATES XERISCAPE PRINCIPLES TO MINIMIZE WATER USE.
HYDRIA REPLACES 2 MILLION GALLONS OF WATER EACH
YEAR THAT OTHERWISE WOULD HAVE BEEN OBTAINED
FROM THE POTABLE WATER SUPPLY.

2005

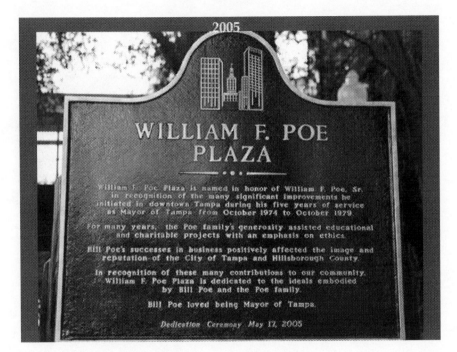

1939

1940-1942

1941 - 1945

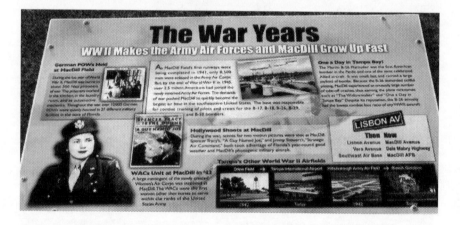

Mac Dill Park

The Memorial to the Seminole Wars, 2003 - 2008

The Memorial to the Seminole Wars depicted above, was dedicated in 2003 and located in another area of the Park. The expansion of the Park required that the memorial be redesigned and moved closer to the natural edge of the water. This also provided the opportunity for additional input from scholars and tribal leaders, and created more continuous open space for all to enjoy.

Memorial Design

The plans of the City of Tampa to create a park here, on the last remnant of the old Fort Brooke military establishment, brought into focus the centrality of the site to the history of Tampa & Tampans, the Florida Indians &, indeed, to all Floridians. The events that transpired here fairly demanded that a Memorial should be erected, in honor of the men who were stationed here, the Indians who fought here, & the men, women, and children who lived and died here during the Seminole Wars of Removal, which took place between 1817 & 1858. The Memorial's design, from its fabric to its shape to its text, was conceived of as a single message of honor for those combatants.

The design is organic. The natural materials - limestone & coquina, tie the structure firmly to the Florida land. Native plants enfold the Memorial. Visitors are invited to walk over & around the structure, to recall how firmly the past is tied to the present, & to learn the permanence of its message, as conveyed by the strength of the bronze that carries the text. A sheet of water constantly washes the Memorial, as tears slowly cleanse the past of its pain & bind us all together in a community of shared experiences.

Designer
Collaboration, Inc.

Architect
Rick Penza Architects Inc.

Ceremonial Space

Bob Haozous (Apache, born 1943)

The traditional method of honoring is with an object or image respectfully acknowledging the involved participants and their history. I believe that this park demands an artwork that places importance not only on this history of Florida, but also on concerns for the future of this planet that we all share.

Sited near the old fort, trading and funeral grounds of Tampa, the stainless steel structure Ceremonial Space is a peaceful reflection on the peoples of the past that lived in this area. The intent of this sculpture is to provide the viewer a space for future generations to contemplate our responsibilities to all things that make up our life experience.

Contemporary man is commonly called "the two generation people." This short-range sense of self stands in stark contrast to the Native Indigenous American who commonly had a long-range or seventh generation understanding of responsibility to a place in nature. This continual relationship demands intentional maintenance and continual preparation of that place for the future. The taking care of the earth, maintaining it as you found it and making it a better place for future generations, is a human birthright responsibility. This nature-based and time related wisdom is Indigenous man's offering to modern man.

Ceremonial Space was designed as a reminder that we are all of this earth, canopied by branches of four separate cypress trees. It is a lodge or dwelling structure with four legs forming the primary support for the canopy of the trees, each leg or trunk representing one of the four cardinal directions. These branches separate us from the intensity of the sun and provide us with shade. This simple act of separation symbolize our contemporary beliefs that contradict the notion that we are one with all things. My intent is to present to the public a unifying space that merges our humanity, a space that also offers the wisdom and responsibility of a more meaningful relationship to nature and place. The future vision presented by Ceremonial Space is an ultimate statement of respect, not only for the past and the present, but also for our responsibility to the distant generations of the future.

Heroes Park

"True heroism is remarkably sober, very undramatic..."

CITY OF TAMPA

GLORIOUS PAST
VIBRANT PRESENT
AND
BRIGHT FUTURE